HOT TOPICS

D0841647

INTERNET
SAFETY

Nick Hunter

Chicago, Illinois

www.heinemannraintree.com
Visit our website to find out
more information about
Heinemann-Raintree books.

To order:
☎ Phone 888-454-2279
💻 Visit www.heinemannraintree.com
to browse our catalog and order online.

© 2012 Heinemann Library
an imprint of Capstone Global Library, LLC
Chicago, Illinois

Visit our website at
www.heinemannraintree.com

Edited by Adam Miller, Andrew Farrow, and
Adrian Vigliano
Designed by Clare Webber and Steven Mead
Original illustrations © Capstone Global
Library Ltd.
Picture research by Ruth Blair
Production by Eirian Griffiths
Originated by Capstone Global Library Ltd.
Printed and bound in China by Leo Paper
Products Ltd.

15 14 13 12 11
10 9 8 7 6 5 4 3 2 1

**Library of Congress Cataloging-in-
Publication Data**
Hunter, Nick.
  Internet safety / Nick Hunter.
    p. cm.—(Hot topics)
  Includes bibliographical references and
index.
  ISBN 978-1-4329-4871-9 (hc)
  1. Computer crimes—Prevention—Juvenile
literature. 2. Internet—Safety measures—
Juvenile literature. 3. Internet users—
Juvenile literature. I. Title.
  HV6773.H884 2012
  005.8—dc22   2010046905

Acknowledgments
The author and publishers are grateful
to the following for permission to
reproduce copyright material: Alamy pp.
5 (imagebroker), **6** (photography by david
price), **9** (Kamyar Adl), **10** (Jim West),
15 (Bubbles Photolibrary), **17** (i love
images), **21** (Blend Images), **25** (Bubbles
Photolibrary), **30** (Fancy), **35** (Frank
Herholdt), **41** (© Ross Gilmore); Corbis
pp. **13** (© Klaus Tiedge), **18** (© Ocean),
23 (© Ocean); Getty Images pp. **19** (Justin
Pumfrey), **27** (ColorBlind Images), **28**
(Harold Cunningham), **31** (Kimberly White/
Stringer), **33** (THONY BELIZAIRE/AFP),
47 (Jupiterimages), **48** (Doug Menuez),
48 (Getty Images); Shutterstock pp. **8**
(© YAKOBCHUK VASYL), **37** (© Diego
Cervo), **39** (© Andrey Burmakin), **43** (©
bikeriderlondon), **45** (© terekhov igor), **46**
(© Manuel Fernandes).

Cover photograph of a laptop reproduced
with permission of Alamy (© Form
Advertising).

Every effort has been made to contact
copyright holders of any material reproduced
in this book. Any omissions will be rectified
in subsequent printings if notice is given to
the publisher.

CONTENTS

Some words are printed in bold, **like this**. You can find out what they mean by looking in the glossary.

HOW SAFE ARE YOU?

Imagine walking alone through a strange city. How safe would you feel? You would probably be a little nervous. You know that the city is huge, and you are not really sure where you are. There are certainly lots of great things to do in the city, but you need to be careful about which people you talk to. You also need to make sure you do not end up in a dangerous neighborhood.

By comparison, the Internet might seem like a much more friendly place. All of your friends are there. You can chat online and make contact with people from around the world, play games, listen to music, go shopping, and find almost any kind of information you need.

Although the Internet brings huge benefits to our lives, in many ways it can be just as scary as an unknown city. The Internet connects you to everyone around the world—which also means that almost anyone from around the world could connect to you. Some of these people use the Internet to hurt others and commit crimes.

The Internet gives these criminals access to the information—including your personal information—they need to commit crimes. It also enables them to take on whatever online identity they want, which helps them to avoid being caught.

"It is clear life has changed—the Internet has affected people's lives in many new ways and we don't know where this is headed ... This is a very important, very complex issue for society that is going to be debated for the next 50 years."

Larry Page, cofounder of Google, May 2010, quoted in *The Guardian*

Email crime

Every day, there are news reports about people who have been the victims of Internet crimes. Some of these crimes affect thousands of people. For instance, in October 2009 thousands of passwords from Web-based accounts like Microsoft's Hotmail and Google's Gmail were posted online. Criminals had gathered these details from people who responded to official-looking emails (see pages 32 to 35).

Criminals can use personal details like passwords to commit many crimes. They could use this information to steal people's identities (see pages 22 to 26). Are you one of the many people who use the same password for lots of different websites? If so, criminals could also use a password from one site or **application** (for example, email) to access other sites—maybe even your bank account.

These **scams** are just a few examples of the dangers that lurk in the darker corners of the Internet. This book will look at these dangers and explore some of the issues surrounding them. It will also give you plenty of practical advice on how to stay safe online.

■ Some criminals today know that they no longer need to actually rob a bank. Instead, billions of dollars are stolen through various types of online crime every year.

THE GROWTH OF THE INTERNET—AND ITS DANGERS

As the Internet has developed, the people who commit crimes have adapted, too. This means that the number of threats posed online has grown dramatically.

The rise of the Internet

The history of the Internet is very short. The Internet as we know it was only launched early in the 1990s. In the mid-1990s, the Internet was mainly used by scientists and researchers. As computers became smaller and less expensive, there was a massive growth in the use of email and the Internet during the late 1990s. Since then, Internet use has continued to grow at an amazing pace.

■ Cell phone technology has also developed rapidly, and now incorporates the Internet. Early cell phones such as the one in this photo were a very long way from the sleek **smartphones** of today.

The rise of cell phone technology

The use of cell phones has changed drastically, too. Cell phones were still rare in the early 1990s, and they were only used for making phone calls! But since the beginning of the 21st century, cell phone technology has changed greatly, with more people able to access the Internet through **wireless networks** and smartphones.

Living our lives online

All these changes have made the Internet much more accessible. We can access websites on the move or on our phones. This means that we live more of our lives online. The amount of time we spend online increases every year, and more information about us appears on the Internet all the time.

The problem with this is that it creates many more opportunities for **cyber** criminals to track people online and to make use of their personal details to commit crimes.

YOUR DIGITAL FOOTPRINT

What could someone find out about you on the Internet? Anyone who uses the Internet leaves a digital footprint. Try typing your own name or email address into a **search engine** like Google. If you have posted anything in a **forum** (online discussion) using your own name or email address, this would enable someone to find more information about you—for example, your interests and the names of your family and friends. Your profile on a **social networking site** like Facebook could give all sorts of information about you if you do not set limits on who can view information (see pages 30 and 31). You may even find a picture of your house and a map of how to get there.

Creating an identity

One of the key characteristics of the Internet is that people can create different identities for themselves. They can use different email addresses and different profiles or **avatars** (characters or symbols) on websites.

Some people see a positive side to this aspect of the Internet. It gives people the freedom to be whomever they want to be. But the downside is that you often cannot know if the people you are chatting with or emailing are who they say they are. As we will see, many dangerous people use this to their advantage.

The Internet is a global network. This has lots of benefits, but it also causes problems.

CORPORATE CONTROL

Although no single authority can control the Internet, there are a few huge corporations that have come to dominate it, including Google, Microsoft, Apple, and Facebook. These corporations are able to track what people do on the Internet and hold lots of personal information about people and their online lives. Many critics are concerned that these companies know too much about people. They argue that people have a right to more privacy. (For more on this topic, see pages 28 to 31.)

Independent or lawless?

Another characteristic of the Internet is that it is unregulated. Since it began, the Internet and the people who use it have fought to be independent of individual governments. The Internet is made up of millions of different **servers** and computers around the world. It is impossible for one country to control it— although some countries do try to restrict what their citizens can access.

So, no single authority monitors the Internet. This means that everybody can express their views on the Internet and set up a website or upload material to an existing website. Many people see this freedom of expression as one of the great benefits of the Internet. For example, in countries where people are not allowed political freedoms, they have found a way to spread news on the Internet. At the same time, however, this means that there is little control over illegal or unpleasant material on the Internet.

■ Political protestors in Iran in 2009 were able to use new Internet technologies like Twitter to spread news of their demonstrations, despite their government's attempts to stop them. Many people argue that this is one of the most positive results of the freedom of the Internet.

THREATS TO PERSONAL SAFETY

As we have seen, no single authority can control the Internet. This can lead to great freedom of expression. But this lack of control also means that there is often no one to protect people from encountering dangerous content—or dangerous people.

Controversial websites

There are many websites that are intended for adult viewing only. There are also websites that are violent, extreme, or that contain hate-filled political views that most people find offensive. There are also sites with material promoting or even giving instructions for illegal activities involving drugs or terrorism.

■ On the Internet, the views of racists like these neo-Nazis can be made to seem like fact. You need to be aware that not everything said on websites is true, and many websites are strongly **biased** in favor of one point of view.

If found, the creators of websites with illegal content can of course face criminal prosecution. But the people who view these websites can also land in trouble. There are lots of examples of people who have lost their jobs or gotten into trouble at school for viewing this kind of material.

Hijacked links

Sometimes people **hijack** (take over) **hyperlinks** and direct people to unsuitable material. If you find this happening—for example, if you follow a link when you are researching something at school, and it leads to something offensive—you should report it to an adult. Above all, use common sense. If you find material that you are uncomfortable with, close your **browser** and tell an adult.

Filtering software

Given all of the objectionable websites lurking on the Internet, parents, schools, and employers sometimes invest in filtering programs. These programs will track Internet use and websites visited. They can also prevent access to offensive websites. This leads to concerns about **censorship**, however (see the box below).

SHOULD THE INTERNET BE CENSORED?

Some people argue that the Internet should be censored, or controlled, to prevent people from viewing material that might be offensive or illegal. They make the following arguments:

- This material can be harmful to those who view it, and people would be better off if it could not be seen.
- If those people who produce illegal material were censored, they would stop producing it.

But many people are against censorship. They make the following arguments:

- Who would decide what gets censored? If governments were responsible for censoring material, they might ban websites that disagree with their point of view.
- Freedom of speech or expression is a basic human right. Even if we disagree with what someone has to say, we should defend his or her right to say it.

There are strong arguments on both sides. What do you think?

Meeting people online

We all know that in the real world, we need to be very careful about talking to strangers. Talking to strangers on the Internet can be even more dangerous. If you meet someone in real life, it is much easier to check that they are who they say they are. For example, it would be very difficult for a 40-year-old man to pretend to be a 14-year-old girl. On the Internet, however, a person who is claiming to be a 14-year-old girl could be anyone.

There are a small number of adults online who put a great deal of effort into befriending children and young people. These online **predators** are able to pretend to be someone they are not, since the targets they communicate with cannot see or hear them. Their aim is to build the trust of their target until they can arrange a meeting, or gain enough information about their target to possibly track down where he or she lives. In the most extreme cases, these stories can end in kidnapping or murder (see the box below).

CASE STUDY

Social network nightmare

The shocking story of the murder of Nona Belomesoff, from Sydney, Australia, shows the risks of believing what people say on social networking sites. Eighteen-year-old Nona had always wanted to work with animals. Nona thought her dream could come true when she met a man on Facebook whose profile said he worked for an animal welfare group. Christopher Dannevig offered her a job with the organization, and Nona agreed to go with him on a camping trip. But he did not work in animal welfare. He had faked the information on his Facebook profile. Nona was murdered by the man she thought could lead her to a dream job.

Social networking dangers

Think of all the websites you use to chat with people online. Some online criminals find websites like these, which are particularly popular with young people, and use them to make contact.

Many young people belong to social networking sites like Facebook and MySpace. If you use a social networking site, think about the people you meet there. How many friends do you have on your profile? Are they all really your friends? Do you know them outside of the Internet? You should certainly ask yourself if all your "friends" are who they say they are, and think carefully before adding new friends whom you have not met or spoken to.

Chat rooms are another place where Internet predators will try to find targets. Although many of these chat rooms are monitored and moderated for unsuitable content, this will not stop dangerous people from trying to befriend teenagers by acting like teenagers themselves. Chat rooms linked to online games are another dangerous area (see pages 14 and 15).

■ Are the friends you meet online really who they say they are?

CASE STUDY

Gaming dangers

Internet games are a lot of fun. Sharing the games with friends, including chatting about cheaters or strategies in online chat rooms, are big reasons why so many people get involved in **MMORPGs** (Massive Multiplayer Online Role-Playing Games) like *World of Warcraft*. However, it is important for people to follow many of the same rules they would for other areas of the Internet, like social networking sites, as this story shows.

Steve and *World of Warcraft*

Like many 14-year-olds, Steve loved gaming. His favorite game was *World of Warcraft*, and he would play it for hours every day, chatting with friends online about the game and life in general. Steve's passion for gaming helped him to deal with a tough time he was having at school. He was being bullied and struggling with his schoolwork.

Online friendship

Steve started talking to someone named Kevin online. Kevin really seemed to understand what Steve was going through, and they spent a lot of time chatting online. After a while, they exchanged email addresses and phone numbers. Steve did not even think it was strange when Kevin started asking him some very personal questions.

After a while, Kevin suggested that Steve should come to stay with him. Kevin's parents had even bought a plane ticket for Steve, which seemed very generous. Steve packed his bag and headed to the airport. He did not tell his parents. When he arrived at his destination, Kevin suggested that they meet at a hotel rather than his house. Steve was on his way there when he was picked up by the police.

Steve's parents had found he was missing and told the police. The police discovered that "Kevin" was actually a 44-year-old man. Steve had been so pleased to find a friend whom he could talk to online that he had not asked many questions about whether Kevin was who he said he was. Fortunately for Steve, he was not hurt, but things could have been much worse.

What did Steve do wrong?

Look at Steve's story. What mistakes did Steve make to put himself in such danger? Here are a few mistakes he made:

- You should never give out personal details like your email address or phone number to someone you meet online. You should also not give information about your family and where you live.
- Steve's emotional state meant that he ignored warning signs that Kevin may not be who he said he was, such as when he asked personal questions, or when Kevin's parents supposedly bought Steve a plane ticket.
- The biggest mistake Steve made was agreeing to meet with Kevin on his own and not telling anyone where he was going.

Decisions you make about online safety are often tied up with your own emotions. You need to follow these rules so that you do not put yourself in dangerous situations.

Steve should have suspected something was wrong when a person he'd never met bought him a plane ticket. Sometimes emotions stop us from thinking clearly about our own safety.

Avoid real-life meetings

As the stories in this chapter have shown, the dangers other Internet users pose to your personal safety are very real. But there are things you can do to keep yourself safe.

First and foremost, you should never agree to meet someone you have only chatted with online. This is one of the most important rules for staying safe online. If you are convinced that someone is trustworthy and you agree to meet for the first time, talk to the person on the phone first, arrange to meet during the day in a public place, and never go alone.

Safe social networking

Sites like Facebook and MySpace have hundreds of millions of users. These sites are fun, but you need to be smart about them. You should understand the **privacy settings**. It is best to restrict your profile so it can only be viewed by those whom you accept as friends. (For more on this topic, see pages 30 and 31.)

There is lots of pressure on these sites to have as many friends as possible, but you should be selective about whom you accept as a friend. Also remember that if some advertisers and businesses try to make friends with you, they really want to get information about you and try to sell you things.

Protect your identity

Another step you can take to protect yourself online is to make sure that the screen name you use on **instant messaging (IM)** and other online applications does not give away too much information about you. You should especially try to make sure it does not tell people your sex, age, or where you live. A striking screen name may seem like a good idea, but it can also attract attention from the wrong kind of people.

In addition to guarding the privacy of your online profile, you should be careful about what you put online in the first place. Don't post any information that might identify where you live. This obviously includes your address, but also things like your school or any clubs you belong to. Also think carefully about any photos you want to post online.

Look closely at new online friends

Be wary of new online friends. Do all you can to see if they are who they say they are. Do your friends know them? Put their name into a **search engine** to see what comes up.

In addition to the advice in this chapter, trust your instincts about whether someone is genuine. If you are concerned about people you meet online, talk to an adult about it.

WEBCAMS

Webcams are great for seeing your friends while you talk to them online. But you should be very careful about when and how you use webcams. Online predators will often encourage their victims to use webcams. If anyone asks you to do anything on a webcam that you are uncomfortable with, it is important that you speak to an adult.

■ Webcams can bring many benefits, but online predators can take advantage of them.

CYBER BULLYING

Have you ever received a nasty text message, IM, or email? If you have, you are not alone. Bullying has always been a problem for many young people, but the Internet has given bullies a new way to reach their victims. Any bullying that happens through the Internet or other electronic communication, such as cell phones, is called **cyber bullying**. Cyber bullying can be very serious, and some victims have been driven to switch schools or even to take their own lives.

Traditional bullying usually happens at school or in public. There is no escape from cyber bullying, though, because it comes into your home through your phone and computer.

Weapons of a cyber bully

The most common types of cyber bullying are threatening or hurtful messages that can be sent by text message, IM, or email. Nasty messages can also be posted on social networking sites. It is very easy to set up an online email or IM account, and those who cyber bully often do this to hide their true identities. Cyber bullies often say things online that they would never say in real life, because they do not have to face their victims and see their reactions.

One of the worst things about any type of bullying is that the victim is humiliated in front of friends and bystanders. With cyber bullying, this humiliation can be even more extreme. Cyber bullies may spread false rumors about their victims by email or online. They may also set up websites attacking their victims, often including photos that have been altered to make them rude or embarrassing. These sites can be viewed by anybody.

CASE STUDY

Cyber bullying ends in tragedy

Holly was just like any other 15-year-old. Like most teenagers, Holly used social networking sites to connect with her friends. Friendship was very important to her. But life became unbearable for Holly when she received a series of abusive messages on her Facebook page and by text message.

Holly had made some things up to impress her friends, as many people do. When these stories were exposed as fake, the abuse became unbearable for Holly. She took her own life. After her death, Holly's parents said she "struggled to cope with the huge pressures placed upon her by the modern complexities of 'friendship groups' and social networking."

■ Bullying text messages can be more hurtful than spoken comments because they are written down for the victim to read again and again.

Who are cyber bullies?

A cyber bully could be someone you know, or it may be someone you don't know at all. Internet **trolls** are one example. They are people who deliberately try to make others angry online. They try to cause trouble on the Internet by being rude and argumentative in chat rooms and elsewhere.

Dealing with bullies

Beating cyber bullies is not easy, especially since attacks often use a combination of text messages, IM, and websites. As with many areas of Internet safety, privacy and not sharing too much information are very important parts of protecting yourself from cyber bullies. Only give your phone number to people you know and trust. Only allow friends to access your profile on social networking sites.

Don't be a bully yourself

Be careful what you say and do online. You may not mean to be bullying someone, but jokes can end up not seeming funny when they are written in an email or on a website. Before you forward a teasing message or picture to a friend, think about the effect this may be having on the person being bullied.

PASSWORDS

You should never give your passwords or **Personal Identification Number (PIN)** to anyone else apart from your parents. Never write them down where they could be found. Even if you give your password to a trusted friend, there is no guarantee that it will not fall into the wrong hands in the future.

There are lots of examples of people who have been cyber bullied from their own email accounts. If cyber bullies have the password, they can access someone's account and send nasty emails to that person's friends, pretending to be the victim. This will turn the friends against the victim.

What if I'm being cyber bullied?

Cyber bullying takes many different forms. Here are some steps to take to deal with the most common types:

Keep the evidence

If you receive bullying texts or emails, save them on your computer or phone. If the bullying continues, you may need them as evidence.

Don't reply

Cyber bullies want you to react to their abuse. If you show you are hurt or angry by replying, that will make them feel better. They also may be trying to get a reaction from you, with the aim of getting you barred from a website or chat room.

Block the senders

You can block email addresses or phone numbers that send you the messages. However, it will be relatively easy for a determined cyber bully to start using another address or phone number. If that happens, you can contact your **Internet Service Provider (ISP)** or phone company to trace or block the people sending bullying messages or calls.

Talk to someone

Cyber bullying can be very painful and personal, but you should let a parent or someone at school know what is happening. Cyber bullying is illegal in some places and, if it continues, the school authorities and police will need to get involved.

Surveys say that more than one in four teenagers have experienced cyber bullying.

IDENTITY THEFT AND PRIVACY

Alicia had recently turned 16. She was applying for her first job at a major department store in her home city of Chicago, Illinois. As the store checked into her background, Alicia discovered that someone had stolen her social security number (her government-issued identification number) and been using it since she was 11 years old.

A Chicago man was later charged with this **identity theft**. He had used Alicia's social security number for many things, including securing a loan to buy a house. Although his crime had been discovered, it still had an impact on Alicia's life. The confusion created meant that Alicia was unable to find a job, and she was also refused a cell phone contract. But identity crimes can have even more serious results than that.

GANGS AND IDENTITY THEFT

Criminal gangs can also steal identities. They use lots of different names and identities to obtain money that they have no intention of repaying. They can use this money to fund all sorts of crime, including terrorism and drug trafficking.

What are identity theft and identity fraud?

Alicia's story is just one of millions of examples of identity crimes that happen every year. Identity theft happens when criminals steal other people's identities by using their personal information as if it is their own.

These details can include a victim's name, date of birth, address, mother's maiden name (the last name a mother had before she was married), social security number, and other information like passwords or bank account details.

Crimes committed using stolen details or someone else's identity are called **identity fraud**. Types of identity fraud crimes include buying things online using stolen credit card details, using someone else's identity to get a job, and even inventing a whole life with the stolen identity.

The money made from identity fraud is often used to fund other types of crime.

Young people and identity theft

But why would anyone try to steal the identity of people under 18 years old? Surely it would be better to target adults, who have jobs, bank accounts, and credit cards?

It is true that adults can suffer more if their identities are stolen, since they can also lose a lot of money. But identity thieves do like to target young people. They can more easily create a false identity using a young person's details because they are starting with a clean slate.

CHECKLIST FOR PROTECTING YOUR IDENTITY

✓ Never give your password to anyone else, and have different passwords for all the different sites and services you access online.

✓ Protect your computer against **viruses** and other things that will harm it or steal your personal **data** (information) (see pages 36 and 37).

✓ Destroy all documents that contain personal information using a paper shredder.

✓ Do not include any personal details, such as your address or date of birth, on a website or social networking profile.

✓ Never give personal details to someone you don't know, especially if you receive a phone call or email that you are not expecting.

✓ Always question why you are being asked for personal information. If in doubt, keep your information to yourself.

✓ Check that any website where you are giving personal information is secure (see page 39).

✓ When using an automated teller machine (ATM) or anything that requires a PIN, always cover the keypad as you type in your PIN.

✓ Do not include unnecessary information, like your social security number or driver's license number, when applying for a job.

How many people are affected by identity theft?

In 2009, 11.1 million people were affected by identity theft in the United States alone. It is probably the most common crime on the Internet. Identity theft can cost a lot of money, and it often takes a long time for people to find out that their identity has been stolen.

■ Any documents with personal information on them could be useful to identity thieves. Make sure you destroy them, so that they are unreadable.

Am I a victim of identity theft?

On average, it takes over a year to discover identity theft. What are the signs that you and your family should look out for?

- Carefully check any bank and other statements or bills for transactions that you do not recognize.

- Be aware if mail containing important documents is lost or arrives later than expected. It may have been sent to another address instead.

- Be alert as to whether your garbage has been stolen or tampered with. Identity thieves often look for bills and other important documents in the garbage.

Once you uncover identity theft, it can take some time to untangle all the issues it creates, but you should contact the police as soon as possible.

Consequences

Identity theft can affect people's lives for a long time after they discover that it has happened. Their problems begin with reclaiming money that may have been stolen. As in the case of Alicia, it may make it difficult to get a job or other things that involve official checks, like cell phone contracts or college applications. Victims may also be contacted about the crimes committed by the person who has stolen their identity.

INTERNET ON THE MOVE

Today, many people access the Internet using different gadgets. Although many of the examples and suggestions in this book refer to people accessing the Internet on computers at home, it could equally apply to smartphones and other mobile devices. If you are accessing the Internet and email on the move or in public places, it becomes even more important that you have secure passwords for each application—and these passwords should not be stored on your phone. Phones are much more likely to be lost and stolen than a desktop computer or even a laptop.

Loss of privacy

Sharing too much information on the Internet can lead to issues beyond identity theft. Many people worry that the rise of Internet use is connected to a loss of privacy. We all have things that we want to keep private. You should guard your own information but also respect other people's right to privacy.

Sharing too much on social networking sites

Sometimes this loss of privacy is people's own doing. This is the case when people are too free with personal information, such as sharing photos on social networking sites. Before you upload photos, think about who might be viewing them and whether the photos are appropriate. Would you be happy for your mom, your principal, or a future employer to see the photos you have online?

■ Would you want to share all the photos you show your friends with your teachers or parents?

Colleges and companies often check candidates' social networking sites and, once something is posted, it can be very difficult to remove it completely. Your photos could also turn up on other websites where you did not intend them to appear.

WHAT'S BEEN WRITTEN ABOUT YOU?

Lots of private information on the Internet can come back to haunt you. There is probably lots of information about you on different parts of the Internet, even without you adding any of that information yourself. Try typing your own name into a search engine and see what comes up.

Internet companies: Collecting your personal data

While actions like posting questionable photos are a choice people make, sometimes Internet companies make decisions about customers' privacy that customers do not fully understand.

■ The service "Google Street View" has caused controversy because people have been caught on camera without their knowledge. Is this an example of a corporation putting profit ahead of privacy?

Companies like Google and Amazon want as much information about people as possible. They keep data about what sites people visit and what they buy. They do this because this knowledge will help them try to sell things to customers. If they know what the customers like, they can sell things in a more effective and targeted way. This kind of practice is not just on the Internet. If people have a loyalty card at a favorite store, the store will know exactly what that person buys, how often, and how much.

Stores say this makes it easier for them to serve customers' needs. Similarly, Internet companies argue that if people don't like their privacy policies, they can always choose not to use their services. What do you think?

INTERNET COMPANIES AND PRIVACY

The biggest Internet companies have users all over the world. Governments cannot control them, and so the companies do not always need to worry about the concerns of privacy groups. Moreover, it is in the interest of the companies for people's information not to be private. If companies hold personal information, they can make money from it—for example, by selling advertising.

This is the reality of privacy on the Internet. Still, do you think it is right that services like Google and Facebook determine the level of privacy they offer? People who support the basic right to privacy would argue that these companies need to give more control to customers when it comes to privacy issues. They believe that privacy is a right, not a privilege.

But many Internet companies make the following arguments:

- Most Internet websites are free. They provide a service, so in return they should be allowed to make money—for example, by selling users' information to advertisers.
- Loss of privacy is a small price to pay for the benefits people get from companies like Google, Facebook, Microsoft, and Apple.
- If users are not happy, they have every right to choose another website instead.
- A person can't blame companies because he or she didn't bother to read the companies' privacy policies.

What do you think?

CASE STUDY

Facebook and privacy

On July 21, 2010, the social networking site Facebook announced its 500 millionth user. This meant that 1 out of every 13 people on Earth had a Facebook page. Facebook has become a powerful tool for people to keep in touch with friends, as well as for groups to campaign on all sorts of issues. It is also increasingly becoming a great way for businesses to reach their customers.

As Facebook has grown more popular, some groups have questioned the site's approach to privacy and personal information. These people feel that Facebook is willing to share too much of its users' personal information with other users, and also with businesses.

Privacy settings

Some information on Facebook is always available to everyone, including your name, your profile picture (if you have one), any networks you have joined, and whether you are male or female. But many users share much more than that, including information about home, school, and clubs they belong to.

■ A survey in 2010 found that one-third of young women ages 18 to 34 who use Facebook check the site as soon as they get up in the morning.

Not long ago, people who supported privacy rights believed that Facebook's **privacy settings** were too complex, which resulted in people sharing more information about themselves than they intended to. To begin with, the **default** settings for privacy—meaning the settings people automatically start with—tended to make information public. Some people said that Facebook did not make it clear enough that people needed to change these settings to gain more privacy.

Facebook's response

In 2010 Facebook made an attempt to respond to these concerns. It reduced the amount of information that was publicly available. It also simplified its privacy settings. This change would make it easier for people to decide what they wanted to share. The company said it was responding to users' concerns, and that its aim was to help people share as much information as they wanted to.

For the simplified privacy settings on Facebook to be useful, however, people still have to check their own settings. One of the concerns of privacy supporters is that people will not make the effort to take this step. They hope to educate people about privacy concerns, however, and recommend that people set their settings so that only friends can view personal details.

Why did Facebook act on privacy?

All companies, whether they have 500 or 500 million customers, need to listen to the concerns of their customers. Any publicity about people coming to harm because of information on Facebook would have been bad for the company.

Internet and social networking companies also know that it is very easy for people to switch to another service. In late 2010 a group of young programmers from New York launched a site called Diaspora. The site has been designed as a "privacy–aware, personally–controlled" social network. Time will tell whether challengers to Facebook will ever catch up with it, but safety on social networking sites will be a concern for some time to come.

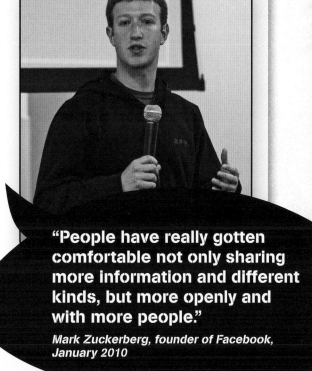

"People have really gotten comfortable not only sharing more information and different kinds, but more openly and with more people."

Mark Zuckerberg, founder of Facebook, January 2010

PHISHING, SCAMS, AND VIRUSES

Anyone who has used email knows about **spam** emails that can clog up your In-box. Spam is not just annoying, however. As we will see, it can also be dangerous.

Spam and similar dangers affect more than just desktop computers and laptops. Any device able to receive email can be a target for these dangers, including cell phones and smartphones. **Viruses** have even been developed that can attack phone **operating systems**.

Spam! Spam! Spam!

Spam emails are sent to millions of people at random. The latest estimates are that around 120 billion spam emails are sent every day. These are getting more and more dangerous, as most now include links that spread viruses and **malware** (see pages 36 and 37).

Blocking spam

How can you prevent spam? Most **ISPs** will provide a filter so that most spam does not reach you. These filters will miss some spam emails, but if you mark these emails as spam, the filter's settings will adjust and should pick up similar emails in the future. You can also set up a separate email address that you use when asked for an email address by an online company. This will keep your main email address private.

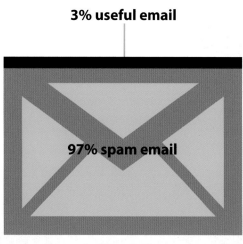

3% useful email

97% spam email

■ Experts estimate that at least 97 percent of all the emails people receive are spam.

Gone phishing

Some of the most dangerous spam emails are those that try to steal a person's personal details through **phishing**. Phishing emails usually contain a hyperlink that directs people to a fake website, which looks like the website of a bank or other trustworthy business. Victims will then be asked to provide information like passwords and **Personal Identification Numbers (PINs)**.

ACT NOW!!?

Phishing emails usually try to get your attention with a call to action. They use phrases that will encourage you to open the email and click on the link. The following are some examples:

- Security Alert—Unauthorized Transaction
- LIMITED TIME OFFER
- Virus Alert

Some will also try to convince you that they are from a friend, so that you will open the email, such as: "Hello, how are you since we met?" These messages are often spelled poorly or contain random characters— for example: "HE2LL%O." Always check the sender of any email before opening it, and never click on a hyperlink unless you trust the sender.

Phishing **scammers** have been known to take advantage of disasters such as the earthquake that struck Haiti in 2010. Some people sent phishing emails that took advantage of the situation and posed as charities.

Pharming

Pharming is similar to phishing, but it does not involve email. In a pharming scam, criminals create a false website that is very similar to the site of a genuine company. They gain access to the genuine website and redirect all users to the fake one, which they then use to collect personal information. Fortunately, pharming is still quite rare.

Fake websites will aim to look like the genuine website, but they will be slightly different. If you look at the top of your browser to see the **URL** (Web address) of the site, it will often be slightly different. For example, http://www.xybank.com may become http://123.xybank.com.

Vishing

Vishing is another variation of phishing. People are asked to provide their details over the phone or to call a number to leave personal details like usernames and passwords. Criminals will then use these personal details online.

Dealing with phishing, pharming, and vishing scams

All these kinds of scams rely on you providing criminals with your personal information. Treat your passwords and PINs as if they were your most valuable possessions, and follow these rules:

- Use a spam filter to protect you from spam and phishing. Improve the filter by marking any unwanted emails that get through as spam.

- Don't open an email unless you know the sender.

- Never reply to any kind of spam email. This will expose you as a good target for more spam and phishing.

- Never click on hyperlinks in emails.

- Do not enter personal information like passwords on a website unless you are sure the site is genuine.

- Reputable companies will never ask you to reveal a PIN or password over the phone or in an email.

What if things go wrong?

If you find out that you have given your personal information to a scammer, make sure you get your passwords and PINs changed immediately. If you or your parents lose money from a bank account or on a credit card, you will probably only get the money back if you inform the bank as soon as possible.

If you accidentally click on a hyperlink in a spam email, your computer could get infected with a virus or malware. You should scan your system with up-to-date security software to check that it has not been infected (see pages 44 and 45).

WHAT WOULD YOU DO?

You may think that very few people would fall for a phishing scam. But in a survey in the United Kingdom, when people on the street were asked for their passwords, one in three people was happy to tell the researchers his or her password. A further one in three would give up a password in exchange for a bar of chocolate. If you give your password to anyone, it could be worth a lot more than a bar of chocolate!

■ If something looks too good to be true, it probably isn't true. This is a good rule for spotting scams. Huge lottery prizes that you can claim only if you supply all your personal details and pay a small fee are not likely to be real.

Viruses and malware

Spam can also infect a computer with malware. Malware describes any software that is designed to harm a computer or spy on a computer from within (see the box below). It sends **data** back to the person who created the malware. Malware and viruses can cripple a computer or smartphone and destroy files. More than 80 percent of spam emails contain links that will spread viruses and malware to a computer.

TYPES OF MALWARE

The following are the details of some of the most common types of malware that could infect a computer:

VIRUS

A virus is a piece of software that can reproduce itself and spread to other computers attached to another program. It relies on the program it is attached to and can only be activated when the program is activated.

WORM

A **worm** is like a virus, but it can run and reproduce itself independently, rather than relying on a host file.

TROJAN

A **Trojan**, also called a Trojan horse, is a file pretending to be one thing, but actually doing something else, such as releasing a virus.

SPYWARE

Spyware includes hidden programs that monitor a user's activity, scan for personal information, or enable the computer to be controlled remotely by someone else.

Many virus and malware attacks try to use a trusted website to make them seem genuine. For example, in 2010 a virus was launched that targeted Facebook users. The email subject line was "Facebook password reset confirmation customer support." The virus told Facebook users that their log-in details had been reset and asked them to click on a link to find out their new details. Once people clicked on the link, it downloaded software that would steal their passwords.

To protect yourself from malware, you should ensure that your system has up-to-date security software. New viruses are being developed all the time, but this software will update itself to deal with the latest threats.

Peer-to-peer file-sharing programs

File-sharing (also called "peer-to-peer" or "P2P") sites that allow people to download and share music and movies are very insecure. Many of these are outside the law. They allow people to download music and movies for free, without paying the artists who produced the songs and films.

By joining these sites, people are effectively opening up their computers to access from the Internet. This opens the door for malware and viruses to infect a computer. It is possible to make an entire hard drive accessible over the Internet.

Official groups—such as the organizations that protect the rights of musicians—are on the lookout for people who illegally download music and movies. They can identify the **IP address** of downloaders. If you download media without paying for it, you run the risk of having your Internet access disconnected or even getting a large fine.

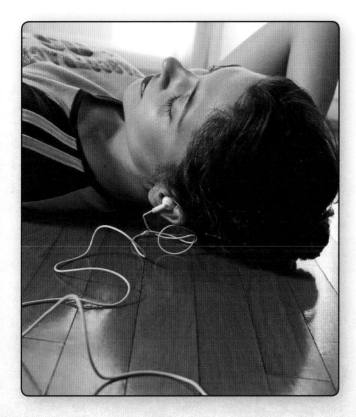

In addition to being a virus risk, downloading music and movies for free can land you in trouble with the law.

MONEY AND SHOPPING

One of the main uses of the Internet is as the world's biggest shopping mall. This has created huge online retailers and marketplaces like Amazon and eBay. It also means that the dangers faced by shoppers in regular stores—such as bank robbers, pickpockets, and more—have been replaced by online criminals and scams.

Trustworthy websites

The first step in safe shopping online is to use trustworthy websites. Use major retailers, since they will have well-established security and privacy policies. If you have to use smaller retailers or websites, check that they have a street address and phone number (not just a cell phone number) on their site, so that you can contact them if anything goes wrong.

CASE STUDY

The eBay approach
Auction sites like eBay deal with millions of individuals who want to sell things on the site. They ask buyers to rate the sellers, so that future buyers can see how trustworthy they are. Pierre Omidyar, the founder of eBay, said, "I founded the company on the notion that people were basically good, and that if you give them the benefit of the doubt you're rarely disappointed."

The vast majority of purchases on online auction sites are successful. Still, you should always beware of fake goods and dishonest sellers on any site.

Be careful when paying

Credit cards are the safest way to pay online. Paypal or another online payment system are also a good option. Always ask before borrowing an adult's credit card, and only use the card on a secure site (see box below). Also, always print and keep a receipt or order confirmation of your purchase.

HOW DO I KNOW IF A SITE IS SECURE?

Whenever you enter personal details or spend money online, you need to know that the website you are using is secure. Any time you send information from one computer to another, it passes through lots of other computers. This means that the information could be read on any of these computers if someone has hacked into their security system. A secure connection **encrypts** this information before it is sent, making it unreadable before it reaches its destination.

To know if a site is secure, you need to look for the following things:

- Check the **URL** of the website. A secure site will begin with "https" rather than just "http."
- A padlock icon should be displayed in the **browser** window. This will normally be in the status bar at the bottom of the window or at the top next to the address bar. Some fake websites will put a picture of a padlock on the Web page itself to give the impression that it is a secure site.

■ Even when you shop in actual stores, you need to closely guard your credit card and personal details.

Registering online

Many online stores and other websites will ask you to register your details before buying something online. If you are asked to register, give the minimum amount of information that the site requires. Never save credit card details as part of your profile. Credit card information can fall into the wrong hands.

As you check out, the website will include a check box that allows you to choose whether you want to receive emails with offers from this company or other companies. This authorizes the company to use your personal information and pass it on to other companies. The wording can be confusing, but read it carefully and choose not to share your information.

Is online shopping safe?

It is certainly much more convenient to buy things on the Internet, especially if, like music, they can be downloaded instantly. For this convenience, people accept a slightly lower level of security than they would get in actual stores. But if we recognize the importance of personal information and do not give it out easily, we can manage the risks.

CASE STUDY

TJ Maxx: Data disaster

While the Internet presents particular dangers, there are no guarantees that credit cards will even be safe in regular stores. One of the biggest losses of **data** in history was discovered in 2007 at the TJ Maxx chain of stores. Thieves were able to **hack** into one of the company's **wireless networks** and, using **malware**, find out the administrative passwords. These, in turn, gave them access to a huge amount of customers' personal data. The thieves may have stolen up to 94 million credit card numbers. Criminals used some of these numbers to create new cards and run up big bills. Other numbers were sold on the Internet.

CONCERT TICKET SCAMS

There are lots of online scams involving concert tickets. Online scammers know that people will go to a website they do not know if it gets them a ticket that is hard to get. So, be very wary of ticket agents, especially if they are selling tickets for an event that everyone else says is sold out. If you buy tickets through these agents, you might very well wait and wait, but never receive your tickets. Odds are that no one will respond to any emails or phone messages you leave with customer service, either. Auction sites like eBay do try to prevent scammer ticket traders, but you cannot always rely on them to catch everyone.

■ Be wary when searching for concert tickets. No concert is worth being the victim of a scam!

PROTECTING YOURSELF

Your gateway to the Internet is your computer. Your computer contains all the details of your identity, and possibly of your family and friends as well. It is important that you keep it safe.

The importance of passwords

Just as you have a key to your house, your various passwords and PINs are the keys to your computer, your phone, and the various applications you use online. As we have seen, it is very important not to give your passwords to anyone.

There are also lots of things you can do to make your passwords more secure. Some passwords are much better than others (see the box below). Passwords are harder to guess if they include numbers and uppercase and lowercase letters, and if they appear to be a random string of characters rather than a word or phrase.

PASSWORDS TO AVOID

Some of the most common passwords are also some of the least secure. Don't use the following, as they will be relatively easy to figure out:

- "password" and any variations like "P@ssw0rd"
- repeated or obvious strings of characters, such as "aaaaaaaa" or "12345678"
- personal information such as your date of birth
- names of pets or family members
- common words or names, as criminals have software that can crack these easily
- obvious replacement characters, such as "0" for "o" or "1" for "i"

Different devices, different passwords

It is also important to have different passwords for each device or application you use. It can be difficult to remember lots of passwords, so there are kinds of software that can manage your passwords for you. The other option is to write them on a piece of paper that is locked away somewhere. This will not be accessible to anyone online.

Cell phone safety

For many people, their cell phone contains almost as much information about them as their computer. It is also much more likely to get lost or stolen. If possible, make sure your phone has a PIN that no one else knows. The advice about using different passwords and not saving them is just as important for your phone. If you lose your phone or it is stolen, you should report it immediately to your phone company.

AVOID SHORTCUTS

You may be offered the option to save passwords or to have forms auto-completed online. This can save a few seconds when you log on to a website, but it can also be dangerous. Anyone who gets access to your computers can log on to your email or another website automatically. You should never use this option on a computer that is used by other people, such as a school computer.

■ Public wireless networks are also very insecure and should not be used for sending any personal information.

Firewalls

As we have seen, up-to-date antivirus software is essential to safeguard your computer from malware (see pages 36 and 37). A **firewall** is another essential feature. This is a program that prevents computers from being accessible to **hackers**. A firewall will be included with most security software.

Still, it is important to remember that a firewall will not protect your computer if your firewall has been disabled or switched off, or if another computer has permission to access yours. This may be the case if you use peer-to-peer file-sharing programs (see page 37). A firewall will also not offer protection if your computer has been infected with a virus that can get around the firewall.

In addition to a firewall, you should always keep your operating system, such as Windows, updated with new updates and **security patches**. These updates are developed to deal with any security issues that are discovered.

Cookies

Your Internet history can be tracked by the websites you visit. **Cookies** are files that are created on your computer when you visit certain websites. They give information about how you used that site—for example, what you have looked at before. As a result, the way the website appears in the future will highlight those features.

In some cases cookies are useful, but you should also be wary of them. You can set your browser to only accept safe cookies. These are ones that do not use any personal information that could be linked to you.

Botnets

There are probably millions of computers around the world that are being used to perform cyber crimes without their owners' knowledge. These are computers that have been infected with a piece of malware that hijacks them, placing them under someone else's control. A network like this, which could include thousands of computers, is called a **botnet**.

Botnets are used to send spam, viruses, and phishing attacks. Your computer could be part of a botnet if it runs very slowly or keeps running when you are not using it. This could also be true if you have items in your sent mail folder that you did not send. Botnets are yet another example of the importance of keeping all your security settings up-to-date.

How a botnet works

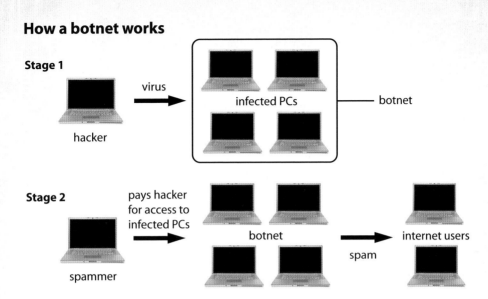

Stage 1

hacker → virus → infected PCs — botnet

Stage 2

spammer → pays hacker for access to infected PCs → botnet → spam → internet users

■ Botnets use thousands of computers to send out spam and malware.

ERASING YOUR HARD DRIVE

Just because you delete a file, that does not mean it is erased from your computer completely. Instead, a version of the file remains on your hard drive. This is important to know, especially if you are planning to get rid of an old computer. The only way to erase the hard drive completely is to use software that will overwrite everything on your hard drive, or to physically destroy the hard drive itself.

TOO MUCH TIME ONLINE?

The Internet has revolutionized many aspects of modern life. But many people believe that there is such a thing as Internet addiction, and that too much time spent online can damage people's health. Is it really possible that an "always online" lifestyle could be damaging to human health?

A recent survey found that one in eight people in the United States showed signs of too much Internet use. Many people stayed online longer than they meant to, often gaming or in chat rooms. For example, once players really get into a MMORPG game (see page 14), it can be very difficult to switch it off and leave to do something else.

Striking a balance

Internet use can become a problem if it affects how much a person is sleeping. There is lots of research saying that teenagers need more sleep than adults, and that not getting enough sleep can affect their ability to concentrate at school and cause irritability.

People need balance in their lives, and if online gaming or social networking takes up too much time, that will affect relationships with others. It will also take away from spending time with other people and from doing other important things, like getting some exercise.

If you feel that spending too much time online is having an impact on other areas of your life, set some strict limits on your Internet use. You can also talk to a parent or teacher about it.

People need to balance the time they spend online with important things like exercise.

CASE STUDY

Gaming addiction

In 2005 a man in South Korea died after playing an online game for 50 consecutive hours in an Internet café. The man died of heart failure because he barely ate or slept during his marathon game. This is an extreme example and certainly not common, but it does show that too much time spent online can have a big impact on health.

ARE YOU SPENDING TOO MUCH TIME ONLINE?

Here are some signs that your Internet use might be causing problems in other areas of your life:

- You spend a lot of time thinking and talking about an online game or website, even when you are not online.
- You prefer to spend time online rather than with your friends.
- You find yourself being more aggressive or argumentative with others due to lack of sleep and lack of time spent with others.
- You feel very tired during the day after an evening spent online, and you find it difficult to keep up with your schoolwork.

Lack of sleep caused by staying online can make you irritable and more likely to argue with friends and family.

DEBATING INTERNET FREEDOM AND SAFETY

As we have seen throughout this book, Internet safety involves some major issues about technology and how it affects our lives. These issues include freedom, censorship, and the role that governments and corporations play in deciding what happens online.

The following are debates raised by the issues discussed in this book, including arguments for and against. Consider the issues and decide what you think about these debates. Can you think of other arguments?

People who commit crimes on the Internet should be banned from it

■ Would banning cyber criminals from going online make the Internet a safer place for everyone else?

Arguments for:

- If people could not use the Internet, they would not be able to commit their crimes again.
- People who commit crimes on the Internet do not deserve to enjoy its benefits.
- If people knew that they could be banned, it would make them think twice before committing crimes on the Internet.
- The Internet would be a safer place if criminals were banned from it.

Arguments against:

- The Internet does not turn people into criminals. If they were banned from the Internet, they would find another way to commit crimes.
- It is very easy to pretend to be someone else online. The criminal could always just create a new identity.

- The Internet is so important to our lives that banning people would be too big a punishment for some less serious crimes.

People under 18 should not be allowed on the Internet without supervision

Arguments for:

- There are age limits used to regulate other things that can be dangerous, such as buying alcohol.
- Some of the dangers on the Internet are so great that young people need to be protected.
- Supervising young people online would prevent much of the cyber bullying of teenagers by other teenagers.
- Many criminals target young people. Crime rates would fall if criminals knew that teenagers were not unsupervised online.

Arguments against:

- If young people know about the dangers, they can take care of themselves.
- Teenagers need to learn how to use the Internet safely.
- Denying young people free access to the Internet will have a negative effect on their education.
- Young people do not usually commit crimes on the Internet. Why should they be punished?
- This would be too difficult for police, since people access the Internet in so many different ways, including on their phones.
- Social networking sites already have age limits, but they are not enforced.

The future of Internet safety

In the early 1990s, very few people had even heard of the Internet, let alone used it. Since then, the growth of electronic communication has made it easier than ever before to share our lives with people around the world. Unfortunately, it has also made it easier for some of those people who want to harm us. As technology develops, there will be new threats to our safety, and people will find new solutions to those threats.

Internet safety will continue to be a balance. We must make the best of the opportunities the Internet has to give, while keeping control of information that others could use to commit crimes or harm us.

INTERNET SAFETY CHECKLIST

Safety tip	Will protect you from
Protect passwords: • Never share your passwords. • Have different passwords for different websites and applications. • Use strong passwords that are difficult to guess.	Identity theft, cyber bullying, online fraud
Meeting people: • Never meet people you have met online in person unless you are sure who they are. • Speak to them on the phone before meeting them. • Meet in public and take someone with you.	Online predators
Personal information: • Guard information about yourself as if it were your most important possession. • Choose online names and avatars that don't give away too much about you. • If you are asked for personal details, always question why they are needed. • Don't use auto-complete to fill in online forms.	Identity theft, cyber bullying, online fraud, online predators
Social networking safety: • Understand your privacy settings and only allow friends to see your personal details. • Don't post anything online that you wouldn't want anyone else to see. • Always remember that people who contact you online may not be who they say they are.	Identity theft, cyber bullying, online fraud, online predators
Firewalls and security software: • Make sure your operating system is updated with the latest security patches. • Install antivirus and security software and keep it up-to-date. • Use a firewall and make sure it is enabled.	Identity theft, online fraud, malware, viruses

Safety tip	Will protect you from
Email safety: • Don't open emails if you don't know whom they are from. • Never click on a hyperlink in an email. • Never reply to spam.	Identity theft, cyber bullying, online fraud, online predators, malware, viruses
Peer-to-peer file sharing: • Remember that this leaves your computer open to other users. • Be wary of legal issues about downloading movies and music.	Identity theft, online fraud, malware, viruses, legal issues
Use secure websites: • Don't send any information on an insecure wireless network—for example, in a public place. • Check that websites are secure before buying anything online or supplying personal details.	Identity theft, online fraud, malware, viruses
Protect your cell phone: • Protect your phone with a PIN. • Follow the same rules about personal information as you would on a computer. • If you lose your phone, make sure you report it.	Identity theft, cyber bullying, online fraud, online predators
Use your common sense: • If something looks too good to be true, it probably is. • Think about the risks whenever you are online, and if something does not feel right, shut down your computer and tell someone about it.	All online dangers (when combined with the other guidelines)

GLOSSARY

application computer program designed to do a particular job, such as an email application that is designed to send emails

avatar character or symbol that people choose to represent themselves in an online game or chat room

bias prejudice in favor of one side or the other in an argument

botnet network of computers that have been infected with a piece of malware that hijacks them so they are under someone else's control

browser software application that people use to view, upload, and download files on the Internet

censorship restriction of what people are allowed to see or read

cookie piece of software that automatically tracks a person's activity on the Internet

cyber relating to the Internet or electronic communication. "Cyber" is often added to the beginning of other words or phrases, as in "cyber bullying."

cyber bullying bullying that takes place online or by any electronic means, such as sending threatening emails or text messages

data information

default settings that will be used unless the user changes them—for example, the settings that are first installed

encrypt put information into code so that it cannot be read by anyone apart from the user, or a website the user is sending it to

firewall program that safeguards computers and prevents them from being accessed by hackers

forum online area for discussions where users post topics for discussion

hack get unauthorized access to a computer or network

hacker someone who tries to get unauthorized access to a computer or network

hijack take something over illegally or by force

hyperlink highlighted text that links to a website or another area of the same website

identity fraud crime committed using a stolen identity, such as stealing money

identity theft using someone else's personal information to pretend to be that person, often to commit crimes

instant messaging (IM) way of communicating via messages sent in real time, usually to a group of people on a list of friends

Internet Service Provider (ISP) company that provides the means to connect to the Internet. It may also provide other services like email.

IP address series of numbers that is the unique address for any computer connected to the Internet

malware any software that is designed to harm a computer or spy on it from within, sending data back to the person who created the malware

MMORPG stands for "Massive Multiplayer Online Role-Playing Game," an online game in which thousands of individual gamers compete against each other or work together as teams

operating system basic software that a computer needs to operate, such as Windows or Mac OS

Personal Identification Number (PIN) unique number people use to identify themselves—for example, when taking money out of an automated teller machine (ATM)

pharming fraud in which criminals create a false website that is very similar to the site of a genuine company. They gain access to the genuine website and redirect all users to the fake one.

phishing fake emails asking for personal information such as passwords and bank account details

predator on the Internet, someone who seeks to harm others, particularly young people

privacy settings settings on a website, such as a social networking site, that determine what information others can see about a person

scam trick or fraud, designed to mislead someone

scammer person or organization who tricks and deceives others for their own gain

search engine website, like Google, that enables people to search the Internet

security patch software designed to repair any parts of an application that might be vulnerable to hackers and other security threats

server computer designed to store large amounts of data as part of a network

smartphone phone that is also designed for Internet access and running other applications

social networking site website that enables users to set up profiles of themselves and interact with friends and other users

spam email sent to lots of people, usually advertising a product or spreading malware. Spam is also called junk email.

spyware hidden programs that monitor a user's activity, scan for personal information or enable the computer to be controlled remotely by someone else

Trojan (horse) file that pretends to be one thing but actually does something else, such as releasing a virus

troll someone who deliberately makes comments on websites and in chat rooms that are designed to make people angry and get an aggressive response

URL (Uniform Resource Locator) address of a website, such as www.heinemannraintree.com

virus piece of software that can reproduce itself and spread to other computers attached to another program. It relies on the program it is attached to and can only be activated when the program is activated.

vishing variation of phishing in which criminals use a phone call scam

wireless network network that allows users to connect to the Internet without wires. Wireless networks in public places can be very insecure.

worm piece of software like a virus that can run and reproduce itself independently, rather than relying on a host file

FURTHER INFORMATION

Books

Brown, Anne K. *Virtual Danger: Staying Safe Online*. Mankato, MN: Compass Point, 2010.

Hile, Lori. *Social Networks and Blogs*. Chicago, IL: Raintree, 2011.

Jacobs, Thomas A. *Teen Cyberbullying Investigated: Where Do Your Rights End and Consequences Begin?* Minneapolis, MN: Free Spirit, 2010.

Levete, Sarah. *Taking Action Against Internet Crime*. New York, NY: Rosen, 2010.

Spilsbury, Louise. *Be Smart, Stay Safe*. Chicago, IL: Heinemann Library, 2009.

Wilson, Michael R. *Frequently Asked Questions About Identity Theft*. New York, NY: Rosen, 2007.

Zuchora-Walske, Christine. *Internet Censorship: Protecting Citizens or Trampling Freedom?*. Minneapolis, MN: 21st Century, 2010.

Websites

www.cybertipline.com
The CyberTipline is a U.S. government service for reporting online crimes against young people. You can also call their toll-free number at (800) 843-5678.

www.nsteens.org
This website offers interactive games about Internet safety.

www.connectsafely.org
This website includes tips and forums on various Internet safety topics, including social networking sites.

www.safekids.com
www.safeteens.com
These two related sites provide a wealth of information about cyber bullying and similar topics.

www.wiredsafety.org
This website includes a "Cyber 911 form" for reporting and getting help with problems online.

www.teenangels.com
Visit this website to see how teenagers are helping other teenagers learn about Internet safety.

Topics for further research

Internet security

Many companies and governments spend huge amounts of money tracking what happens on the Internet and protecting themselves and us from cyber attacks. You can investigate how this works and what the threats are.

Online businesses

Many businesses like Facebook and Google have become massive corporations used by hundreds of millions of people in a very short time. Find out more about the people who built these companies. Who are the big winners of the digital age and are there other traditional companies that have lost out?

INDEX